Are you ready for an Art Attack?

Whether it's for a party, school play, carnival or just for fun, dressing up is a creative challenge! Why not have a go at making your own mask or daft disguise? In this book you will find lots of ideas. Just follow the step-by-step instructions for perfect results, or adapt the ideas to make your own original outfits.

So if you're ready to go mask & disguises mad turn the page and let's have some Art Attacks!

CONTENTS

Editor: Karen Brown   Designers: Ant Gardner/Darren Miles
Artist: Mary Hall   Craft Maker: Susie Johns

Ahoy There!

1 Blow up the balloon to approximately the same size as your head. Stand it in a bowl and brush with diluted PVA glue. Cover with five layers of torn newspaper strips. Leave it to dry, then build up a further five layers.

2 When dry, burst the balloon, so you are left with a thick papier maché shell. Cut this in half, to make two masks.

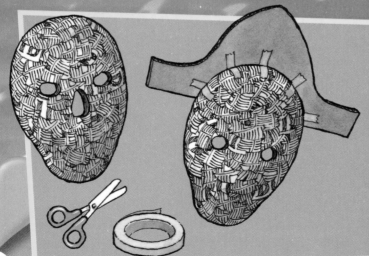

3 Carefully cut holes for eyes. For the pirate mask, add a hat shape, cut from thick card and glued in place to the top. Cut a nose shape in the other mask.

YOU WILL NEED:

round balloon, newspapers,
PVA glue, cardboard,
paints, string.

4 Paint each mask white, to cover up the newsprint and form a good base. Using the pictures of the finished masks on these pages as a guide, paint details such as eyes, mouths and so on.

5 Pierce a hole on either side of each mask and thread with a length of elastic, to hold the mask in place when you wear it.

5

CRAZY CLOWN!

YOU CAN MAKE THIS AS MAD AS YOU LIKE! PAINT IT WITH WILD STRIPES LIKE THIS, AND ADD SOME PAPER FLOWERS, OR CHOOSE YOUR OWN, CRAZY, COLOURFUL DESIGN!

1 Start with a mould that will fit comfortably on your head - a plastic bowl will do! Cover the mould with lots of cling film to protect it and make the finished papier maché shell easy to remove.

2 Cover the mould with about five layers of papier maché and leave it to dry.

3 Make a brim about 5cm wide from a card circle. (It will need to fit over the mould.) Stick the cardboard brim to the mould and cover with another five layers of papier maché. Leave it to dry.

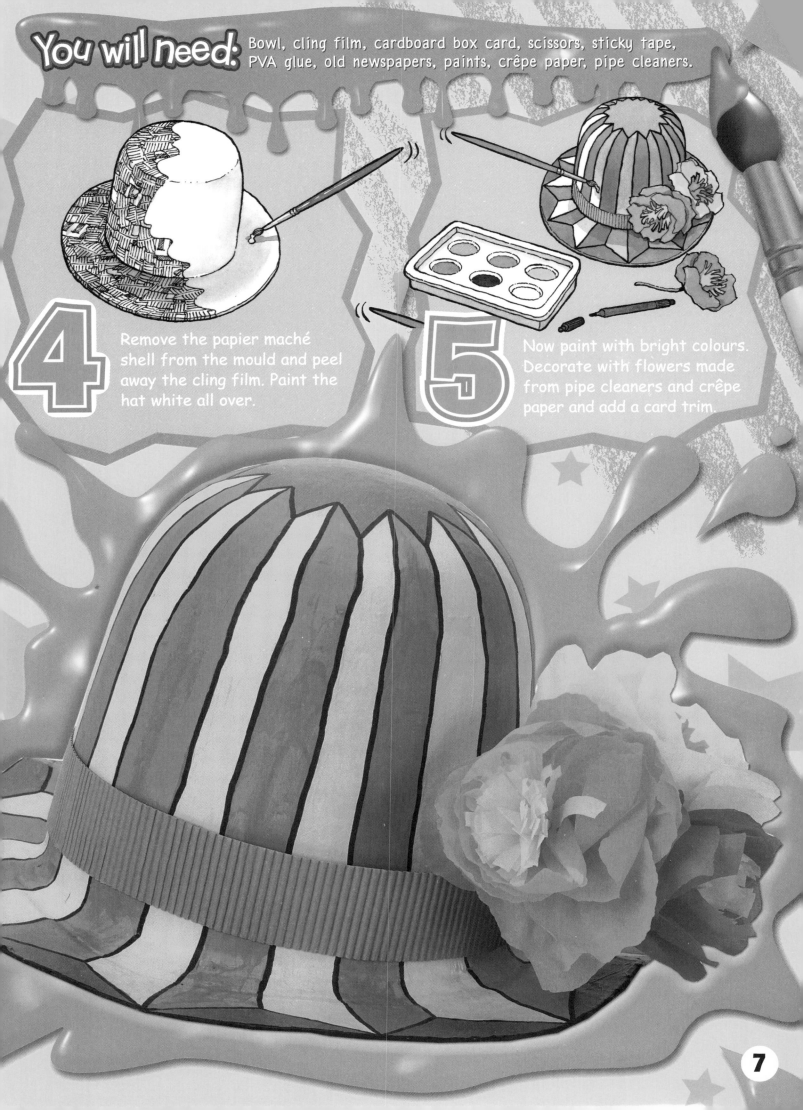

4 Remove the papier maché shell from the mould and peel away the cling film. Paint the hat white all over.

5 Now paint with bright colours. Decorate with flowers made from pipe cleaners and crêpe paper and add a card trim.

If you don't like having a mask fixed to your face, you could just hold this one up to your face when you want to! Why not combine it with the hat or the wig from page 24 for a really funny effect?

YOU WILL NEED:
cardboard box card, scissors, sticky tape, 2 polystyrene cups, ping pong ball, PVA glue, old newspapers, paints, crêpe paper, zigzag or plain scissors.

1 Cut a circle of card 20cm in diameter. Cut the bases from two polystyrene cups for cheeks, cut two cardboard ears, take a ping pong ball for the nose, and stick them all in position.

2 Cover with two layers of papier maché and leave it to dry overnight.

3 Paint the clown white all over - you may need two coats to cover the newsprint. Then paint the details. Pierce holes in the eyes so you can see through the mask.

4 Add some spikey hair. Cut two strips of crêpe paper measuring 25cm x 8cm. Cut each one into a fringe using zig zag scissors if you have any. Tape them to the back of the mask.

BAG IT UP!

These are easy and cheap to make - perfect for a party! Why not make one each for your guests, or have a mask-making session where guests can paint their own?

1 Start with a sturdy paper bag - the kind used for takeaway food is perfect. Snip off any handles and glue cut-out card ears in place on the top edge.

2 Paint this side of the bag white, leave to dry, then draw features with a pencil. Fill in the shapes with colour, then outline with a black marker pen.

3 Don't forget to cut small peep holes so you can see where you are going when you put the mask on your head!

You could even create a different face on each side of the bag - how about a nice face and then a scary face! Just turn it round to give everyone a fright!

HEY PRESTO!

TRANSFORM YOURSELF INTO A MARVELLOUS MAGICIAN WITH THIS MAJESTIC HAT! FOLLOW THE STEPS TO HAVE A MAGICAL TIME!

1 Cut a circle of card about 28-30cm in diameter. Cut a hole in the centre, so it fits loosely over your head. Snip out a few notches in the ring to add a bit of character.

2 Roll a large sheet of thin card into a cone shape and push it through the centre. Snip the edges into small tabs and tape them to the underside of the ring.

3 To make the snake, roll three carrier bags into sausages, bind with sticky tape and tape in place around the cone. Crumple a sheet of newspaper into a ball for the snake's head.

YOU WILL NEED:

Thin cardboard, scissors, sticky tape, 3 plastic carrier bags, PVA glue, old newspapers, kitchen towel, acrylic paints, red pipe cleaner, 2 googly plastic eyes

4 Cover the whole hat with four layers pf papier maché. Use kitchen roll so you can mould it round the snake. Leave it to dry.

5 Paint the hat purple and the snake green. Add details to the snake such as darker green spots to look like scales and large lilac spots all over the hat. Stick a red pipe cleaner on the snake for a tongue.

MONSTER HEAD

THIS IS REALLY BIG! A HUGE MASK TO FIT OVER YOUR WHOLE HEAD - YOU DON'T LOOK THROUGH THE EYES BUT THROUGH THE MOUTH! PAINT YOUR HEAD AS ANY CHARACTER YOU LIKE: A HAPPY FACE LIKE THIS ONE, OR A SCARY, MONSTER FACE. IT'S UP TO YOU!

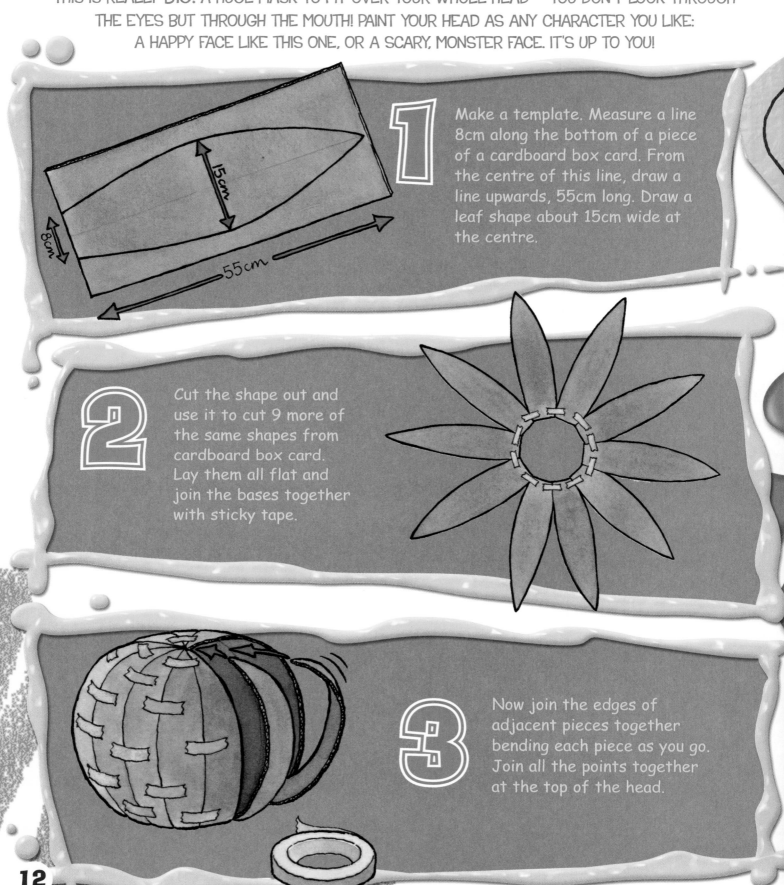

1 Make a template. Measure a line 8cm along the bottom of a piece of a cardboard box card. From the centre of this line, draw a line upwards, 55cm long. Draw a leaf shape about 15cm wide at the centre.

2 Cut the shape out and use it to cut 9 more of the same shapes from cardboard box card. Lay them all flat and join the bases together with sticky tape.

3 Now join the edges of adjacent pieces together bending each piece as you go. Join all the points together at the top of the head.

DS!

YOU WILL NEED: Cardboard box card, scissors, sticky tape, PVA glue, newspapers, paints.

4 Cut ears and a nose out of cardboard and tape them in place. Cut a big slit for the mouth.

5 Cover the whole thing with three layers of papier maché and leave it to dry. Now paint the head.

PUMPKIN HEAD!

WITH SOME MINOR ADJUSTMENTS TO YOUR MONSTER HEAD, YOU CAN CREATE A PUMPKIN HEAD!

THE PERFECT DISGUISE FOR HALLOWEEN! BECAUSE IT'S MADE FROM PAPIER MACHÉ, IT'S SURPRISINGLY LIGHTWEIGHT, DESPITE ITS ENORMOUS SIZE!

YOU WILL NEED:

cardboard box card, scissors, sticky tape, PVA glue, newspapers, paints.

1 Make a template just as you did in step one on the previous page. This time make the centre line 45cm long.

2 Cut out this shape, and draw around it to make eight more shapes. Lay them all flat and join the bases together with sticky tape, to form the neck opening.

3 Now join the edges of adjacent pieces together. Bend each piece as you go. Join all the points together at the top of the head.

4 Cut a big zigzag slit for the mouth. To make the stalk, roll up a scrap of cardboard and glue this in place on top of the head.

5 Cover the construction with at least three layers of papier maché and leave it to dry.

6 Have fun painting the head! Paint it white all over, then, when this is dry, paint it orange. Paint the stalk green and paint triangular, black eyes and nose.

PLATE FACES!

MAKE SIMPLE MASKS FROM PAPER PLATES. HERE ARE THREE IDEAS, BUT YOU CAN THINK UP SOME OF YOUR OWN!

PUSSY

Cut ears and a triangular nose and glue in place on the plate. Cut holes for the eyes. Paint the plate to look like a cat. Make holes either side and tie some elastic in place.

PIGGY

Cut out a large oval shape and stick it on the front to make a nose, attach two card ears. Paint the plate pink and add some brown patches for mud. Make two holes for eyes. Create a face with black paint and let it dry. Make holes either side, attach elastic and it's ready to wear!

PUPPY

Cut long, oval ears and a nose from card and stick in place. Pierce small holes for your eyes. Paint the plate beige with brown patches. Add details with black paint. Finally make holes either side and thread some elastic through.

15

ALIEN MASK!

BECAUSE THIS MASK IS MADE FROM PAPIER MACHÉ ON A THICK CARDBOARD BASE IT IS VERY STURDY AND CAN BE USED TIME AND TIME AGAIN, WHENEVER YOU HAVE THE URGE TO DRESS UP AS A CREATURE FROM ANOTHER PLANET!

1 Fold an A3 piece of paper in half and draw a face. It should be the same length as your face with eyes and a mouth in the same positions as your eyes and mouth.

2 Cut the face template out and tape it to the corner of a cardboard box and draw around it. Draw a straight line across the top. Cut it out and cut out the eye holes.

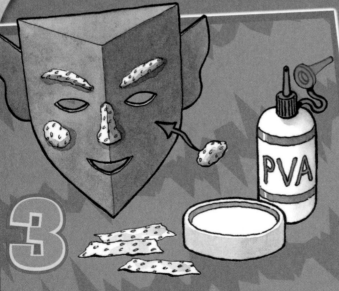

3 To make a nose and eyebrows, dip some kitchen roll in diluted PVA and squeeze out the excess. Press it on to the mask, moulding it into shape with your fingers. You can pad out the cheeks and chin, too.

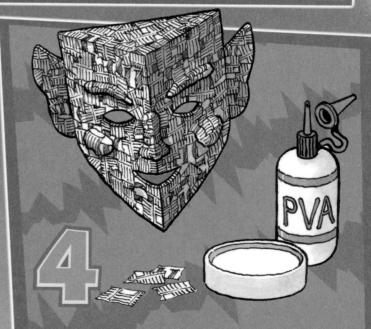

4 Cover the whole mask with three layers of papier maché and leave it to dry until it's rock hard.

5 Paint your alien with a coat of white paint. When dry, paint it different shades of green. Dab a little pink paint on the cheeks. Finally outline the eyes in black marker pen.

6 To make the antennae, push a pencil through the top of the head to make two holes. Fold a pipe cleaner in half, twist it and then thread a pom pom or bead on to the folded end. Push the other end through the hole in the head. Do this for both sides.

CHINESE DRA

1 Trace the basic shape on the opposite page and cut it out from sturdy card.

2 Cut shapes from coloured paper scraps and stick them on to your mask, using a glue stick.

3 Add triangular paper teeth and a long red tongue.

4 For the handle, use a cardboard tube. Cut two slits in one end of the tube and slot the mask in!

NOW YOU HAVE SEEN WHAT TO DO, MAKE SOME DIFFERENT SHAPED MASKS. YOU CAN USE THE SAME TUBE HANDLE.

EYE MASKS!

THESE QUICK AND EASY EYE MASKS ARE PERFECT FOR PARTIES, PLAYS AND DRESSING UP!

BUZZY BEE

BEAUTIFUL BUTTERFLY

1

Trace the eye template from the opposite page and draw around it on to a piece of yellow card.

2

Glue strips of black paper across the shape you have drawn, then cut out around the outline.

3

Trace the wing template, cut two from tracing paper and draw veins in pencil. Stick them in place.

4

For antennae, glue pom poms on the ends of two short pipe cleaners and glue the other ends in place on the mask.

5

Finally, make a small hole either side of the eye piece and thread string or elastic though.

The butterfly eye mask is made in a similar way to the bee, except the wings are cut from card.

Try to find metallic or iridescent card for a shimmering effect. Cut shapes from scraps of coloured paper or card to decorate the wings.

Choose your own colour combinations.

20

FEATHERED HE

THE PERFECT FINISHING TOUCH FOR A NATIVE AMERICAN COSTUME - COLOURFUL HEAD BANDS DECORATED WITH SPLENDID FEATHERS AND FRINGES, OR EVEN SOME HAIR BRAIDS!

ADDRESS!

YOU WILL NEED:
Corrugated card, coloured feathers, sticky tape, coloured paper, crêpe paper, black wool.

1 Measure around your head and cut a wide strip of corrugated card about 3cm shorter than this measurement.

2 If the corrugations are quite large, you may be able to push the stalks of the feathers into the holes. Otherwise, attach the stalks to the wrong side of the band, using sticky tape.

3 Cut a second band and stick it to the first, to cover up the tape and produce a neat result.

4 Cut shapes from paper and stick them on the band, to decorate it. You could also add thin strips of crêpe paper, dangling down.

5 To complete your disguise, why not make plaits from lengths of black knitting yarn. You can clip the ends to your hair, or tape them to the inside of the head band.

MORE IDEAS...

This time cut the corrugated card into a different shape, bend it round, and tape it in position so it fits on your head.

Using sticky tape or staples, attach a single feather at the side.

Cut out a picture of a flying bird and stick it to the front. Stick on other coloured shapes.

FUNNY FACES!

THIS IS GREAT FOR CLOWNING AROUND! MAKE THE HAIR THE COLOUR AND TEXTURE YOU LIKE, USING RAFFIA, STRING OR KNITTING YARN! ADD SOME FUNNY GLASSES FOR COMEDY EFFECT!

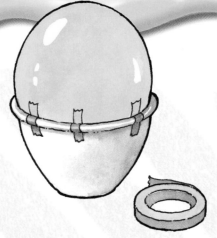

1 Blow up a balloon to approximately the same size as your head. Stand it inside a bowl, taping it in place to keep it steady.

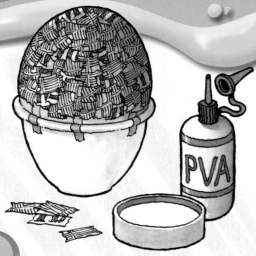

2 Cover just over half of the balloon with four layers of papier maché and leave it to dry.

3 Burst the balloon and remove it from the shell. Trim the edges so you have half a head shape. Paint the shell the colour of your skin.

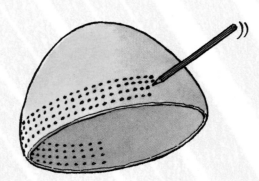

4 Pierce holes all over the bottom half of the shell, where you want the hair to go.

5 Cut short lengths of wool, string or rafia - about 15cm long. Push the ends through two adjacent holes and knot together on the outside; do this until you have lots of hair!

YOU WILL NEED:

Balloon, bowl, sticky tape, newspaper, PVA glue, wool or rafia, card, paints.

MAKE A SPECTACLE OF YOURSELF WITH THE SILLY GLASSES OVER THE PAGE!

1 Trace the glasses and the arms onto card and cut them out.

2 Stick the arms on the sides.

3 Stick on fake jewels, decorate with glitter or just paint.

4 When dry, they're ready to wear!

USE THIS IDEA TO GO AS CRAZY AS YOU WANT AND MAKE YOUR OWN SILLY SPECS!

ART ATTACK

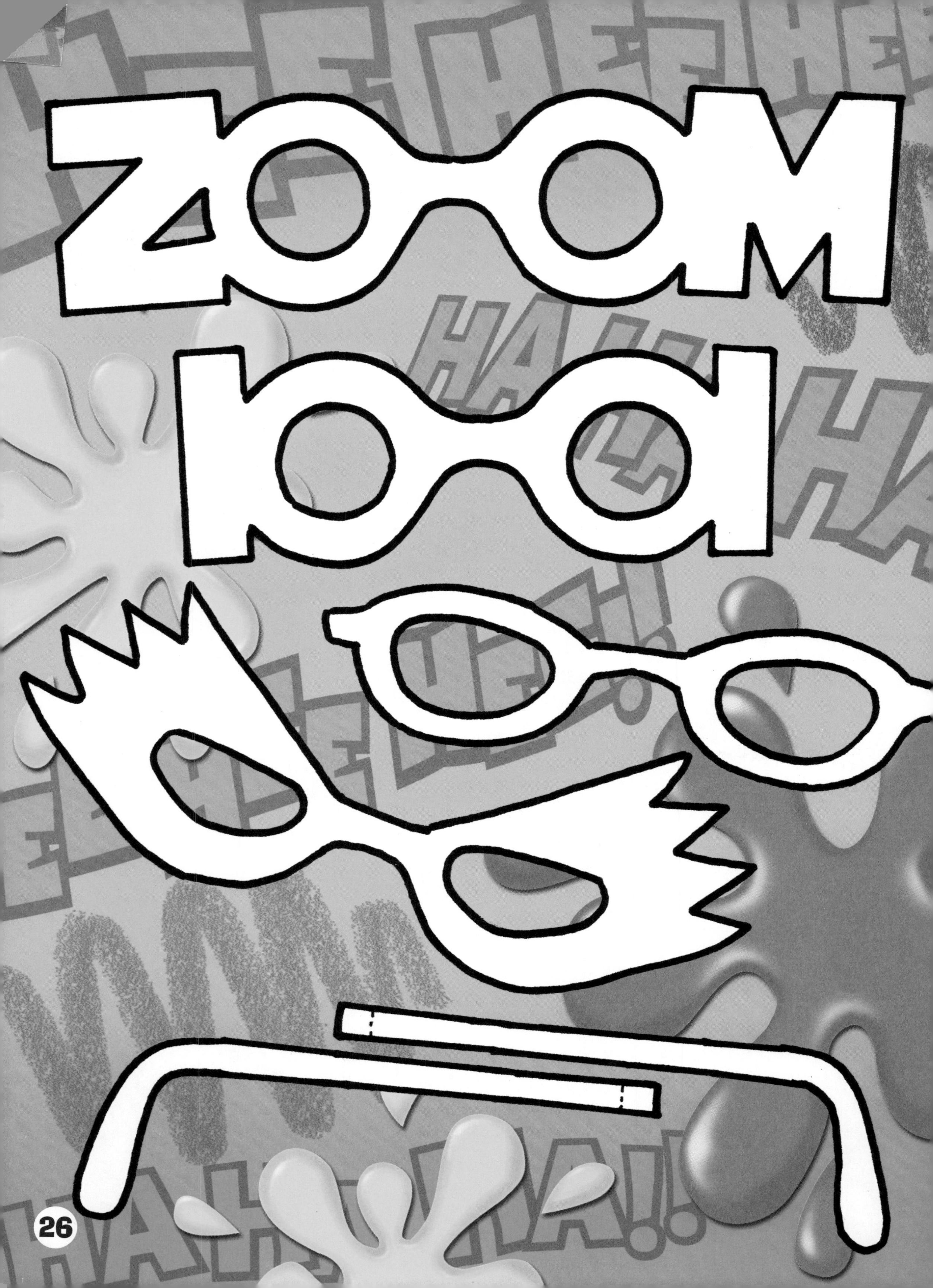
ZOOM